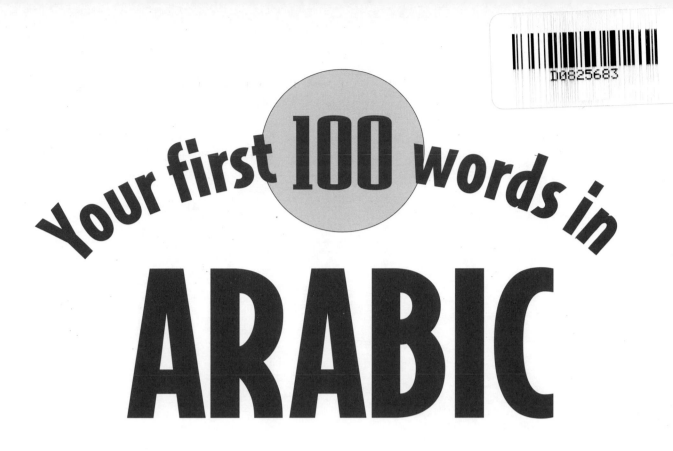

Your first 100 words in

ARABIC

Beginner's Quick & Easy Guide to Demystifying Arabic Script

Series concept
Jane Wightwick

Illustrations
Mahmoud Gaafar

Arabic edition
Mahmoud Gaafar

PASSPORT BOOKS
NTC/Contemporary Publishing Group

Other titles in this series:

Your First 100 Words in Chinese
Your First 100 Words in Japanese
Your First 100 Words in Russian

Cover design by Nick Panos

Published by Passport Books
A division of NTC/Contemporary Publishing Group, Inc.
4255 West Touhy Avenue, Lincolnwood (Chicago), Illinois 60712-1975 U.S.A.
Printed in the United States of America
International Standard Book Number: 0-8442-2395-6

3 4 5 6 7 8 9   VLP/VLP   0 5 4 3 2

◎ CONTENTS

◎ INTRODUCTION

In this activity book you'll find 100 key words for you to learn to read in Arabic. All of the activities are designed specifically for reading non-Latin script languages. Many of the activities are inspired by the kind of games used to teach children to read their own language: flashcards, matching games, memory games, joining exercises, etc. This is not only a more effective method of learning to read a new script, but also much more fun.

We've included a **Scriptbreaker** to get you started. This is a friendly introduction to the Arabic script that will give you tips on how to remember the letters.

Then you can move on to the eight **Topics**. Each topic presents essential words in large type. There is also a pronunciation guide so you know how to say the words. These words are also featured in the tear-out **Flashcard** section at the back of the book. When you've mastered the words, you can go on to try out the activities and games for that topic.

There's also a **Round-up** section to review all your new words and the **Answers** to all the activities to check yourself.

Follow this 4-step plan for maximum success:

1 Have a look at the key topic words with their pictures. Then tear out the flashcards and shuffle them. Put them Arabic side up. Try to remember what the word means and turn the card over to check with the English. When you can do this, cover the pronunciation and try to say the word and remember the meaning by looking at the Arabic script only.

2 Put the cards English side up and try to say the Arabic word. Try the cards again each day both ways around. (When you can remember a card for seven days in a row, you can file it.)

3 Try out the activities and games for each topic. This will re-inforce your recognition of the key words.

4 After you have covered all the topics, you can try the activities in the **Round-up** section to test your knowledge of all the 100 words in the book. You can also try shuffling all the flashcards together to see how many you can remember.

This flexible and fun way of reading your first words in Arabic should give you a head start whether you're learning at home or in a group.

4

◎ SCRIPTBREAKER

The purpose of this Scriptbreaker is to introduce you to the Arabic script and how it is formed. You should not try to memorize the alphabet at this stage, nor try to write them yourself. Instead, have a quick look through this section and then move on to the topics, glancing back if you want to work out the letters in a particular word. Remember, though, that recognizing the whole shape of the word in an unfamiliar script is just as important as knowing how it is made up. Using this method you will have a much more instinctive recall of vocabulary and will gain the confidence to expand your knowledge in other directions.

The Arabic script is not nearly as difficult as it might seem at first glance. There are 28 letters (only two more than in the English alphabet), no capital letters, and, unlike English, words are spelled as they sound. There are two main points to etch into your brain:

- Arabic is written from right to left.
- The letters are "joined up" — you cannot "print" a word as you can in English.

◎ The alphabet

The easiest way of tackling the alphabet is to divide it into similarly shaped letters. For example, here are two group of similar letters. The only difference between them is the dots:

ح (the letter *Haa*)　　　　　ب (the letter *baa*)

ج (the letter *jeem*)　　　　　ت (the letter *taa*)

خ (the letter *khaa*)　　　　　ث (the letter *thaa*)

When these letters join to other letters they change their shape. The most common change is that they lose their "tails":

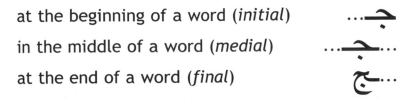

تج = ج + ت　　　حب = ب + ح (read from *right to left*)

Because letters change their shape like this, they have an *initial*, a *medial* (middle) and a *final* form. For example, the letter ج (*jeem*) changes like this:

at the beginning of a word (*initial*)　　　جـ...

in the middle of a word (*medial*)　　　...ـجـ...

at the end of a word (*final*)　　　ـج...

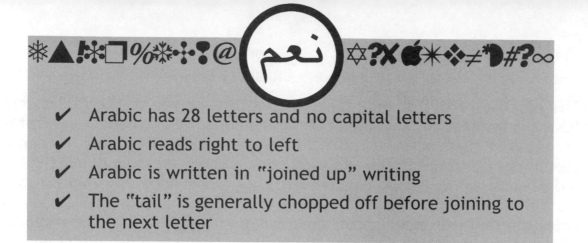

- ✔ Arabic has 28 letters and no capital letters
- ✔ Arabic reads right to left
- ✔ Arabic is written in "joined up" writing
- ✔ The "tail" is generally chopped off before joining to the next letter

A few letters change their shapes completely depending on where they fall in a word. For example, the letter ه (*haa*) changes like this:

initial   ...ﻬ

medial   ...ﻬ...

final   ﻪ...

In addition, there are six letters which *never* join to the letter *following* (to their left) and so hardly change shape at all. These are:

و (*waw*)   ا (*alif*)

د (*daal*)   ذ (*THaal*)

ر (*raa*)   ز (*zay*)

You will find more details of how the individual letters change their shape in the table on page 8.

◎ Formation of words

We can use the principles of joining letters to form words.

So, for example, the Arabic word for "river" (*nahr*) is written like this:

(*nahr*) نهر = (r) ر + (h) ه + (n) ن   ⟵

The Arabic word for "belt" (*Hizaam*), contains two non-joining letters and is written like this:

(*Hizaam*) حزام = (m) م + (aa) ا + (z) ز + (H) ح   ⟵

You may have noticed that some of the vowels seem to be missing from the script. In written Arabic, the three short vowels (*a, i, u*) are not written as part of the script but as vowel signs above or below the letter. The short *a* is written as a dash above the letter (–́); the short *i* as a dash below (–̣); and the short *u* as a comma-shape above (–́). This is similar to English shorthand, where we might write "bnk" instead of "bank." Here are the words for "river" and "belt" again, this time with the vowel signs:

نَهر (nahr)   حِزام (Hizaam)

In this book we have included these vowel signs in the topics, but dropped them in the review section (*Round-up*). Most material for native speakers will leave them out as you are presumed to know them. This makes it all the more important for you to start recognizing a word without the short vowels.

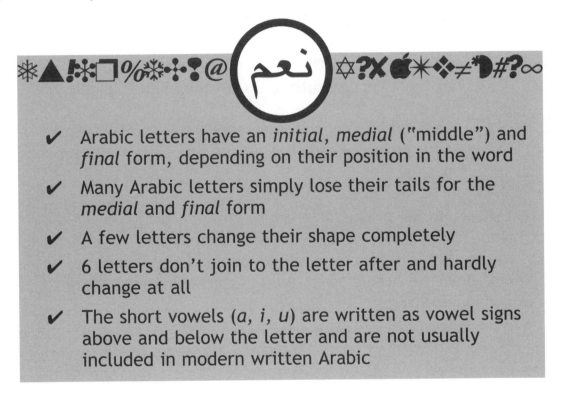

✔ Arabic letters have an *initial*, *medial* ("middle") and *final* form, depending on their position in the word

✔ Many Arabic letters simply lose their tails for the *medial* and *final* form

✔ A few letters change their shape completely

✔ 6 letters don't join to the letter after and hardly change at all

✔ The short vowels (*a, i, u*) are written as vowel signs above and below the letter and are not usually included in modern written Arabic

◎ Pronunciation tips

This activity book has simplified some aspects of pronunciation in order to emphasize the basics. Don't worry at this stage about being precisely correct – the other letters in a word will help you to be understood. Many Arabic letters are pronounced in a similar way to their English equivalents, but here are a few that need special attention:

ص (saad)   a strong "s," pronounced with the tongue on the roof of the mouth rather than up against the teeth

ض (Daad)   a strong "d," pronounced with the tongue on the roof of the mouth rather than up against the teeth

ط (Taa)	a strong "t," pronounced with the tongue on the roof of the mouth rather than up against the teeth
ظ (zaa)	a strong "z," pronounced with the tongue on the roof of the mouth rather than up against the teeth
ح (Haa)	pronounced as a breathy "h"
خ (khaa)	pronounced like the "ch" in the Yiddish "chutzpah"
ع ('ayn)	the sound most often associated with Arabic, and most difficult to produce: a sort of guttural "ah"-sound
غ (ghayn)	pronounced like the French throaty "r"
ء (hamza)	a strange "half letter." Not really pronounced at all, but has the effect of cutting short the previous letter
ة (taa marboota)	a version of (taa) that only appears at the end of words and is pronounced "a"

◎ Summary of the Arabic alphabet

The table below shows all the Arabic letters in the three positions, with the Arabic letter name, followed by the sound. Remember that this is just for reference and you shouldn't expect to take it all in at once. If you know the basic principles of how the Arabic script works, you will slowly come to recognize the individual letters.

	initial:	medial:	final:		initial:	medial:	final:		initial:	medial:	final:
alif a/u/i/aa	ا	ـا	ـا	zaa z	ز	ـز	ـز	qaaf q	ق	ـق	ـق
baa b	بـ	ـبـ	ـب	seen s	سـ	ـسـ	ـس	kaaf k	كـ	ـكـ	ـك
taa t	تـ	ـتـ	ـت	sheen sh	شـ	ـشـ	ـش	laam l	لـ	ـلـ	ـل
thaa th	ثـ	ـثـ	ـث	Saad S	صـ	ـصـ	ـص	meem m	مـ	ـمـ	ـم
jaa j	جـ	ـجـ	ـج	Daad D	ضـ	ـضـ	ـض	noon n	نـ	ـنـ	ـن
Haa H	حـ	ـحـ	ـح	Taa T	طـ	ـطـ	ـط	haa h	هـ	ـهـ	ـه
khaa kh	خـ	ـخـ	ـخ	Zaa Z	ظـ	ـظـ	ـظ	waaw w/oo	و	ـو	ـو
daal d	د	ـد	ـد	'ayn '	عـ	ـعـ	ـع	yaa y/ee	يـ	ـيـ	ـي
THaal TH	ذ	ـذ	ـذ	ghayn gh	غـ	ـغـ	ـغ				
raa r	ر	ـر	ـر	faa f	فـ	ـفـ	ـف				

① AROUND THE HOME

Look at the pictures of things you might find in a house.
Tear out the flashcards for this topic.
Follow steps 1 and 2 of the plan in the introduction.

شُبّاك
shubbaak

كُرسي
kursee

مائِدة
maa-ida

تِليفزيون
tileefizyoon

كَنَبة *kanaba*

كُمبيوتر
kumbiyootir

تِليفون
tileefoon

سَرير
sareer

ثَلاجة
thallaaja

دولاب
doolaab

باب
baab

فُرن *furn*

9

◎ **M**atch the pictures with the words, as in the example.

كَنَبة
سَرير
شُباك
مائِدة
تِلِيفِزيون
كُرسي
كُمبيوتر
تِليفون

- -

◎ **N**ow match the Arabic household words to the English.

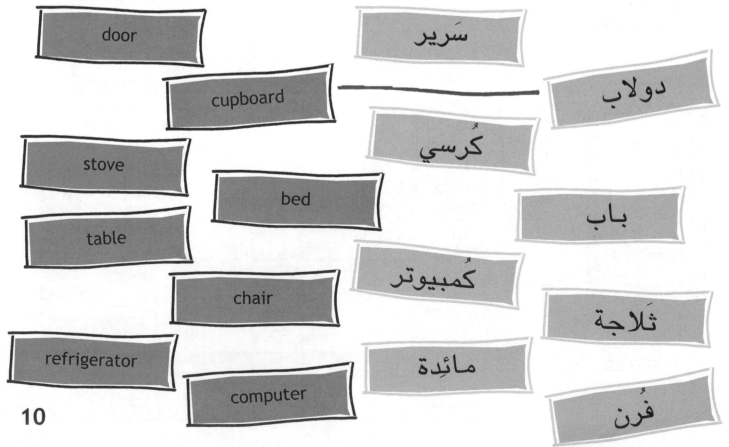

door	سَرير
cupboard	دولاب
stove	كُرسي
bed	باب
table	كُمبيوتر
chair	ثَلاجة
refrigerator	مائِدة
computer	فُرن

10

◎ **M**atch the words and their pronunciation.

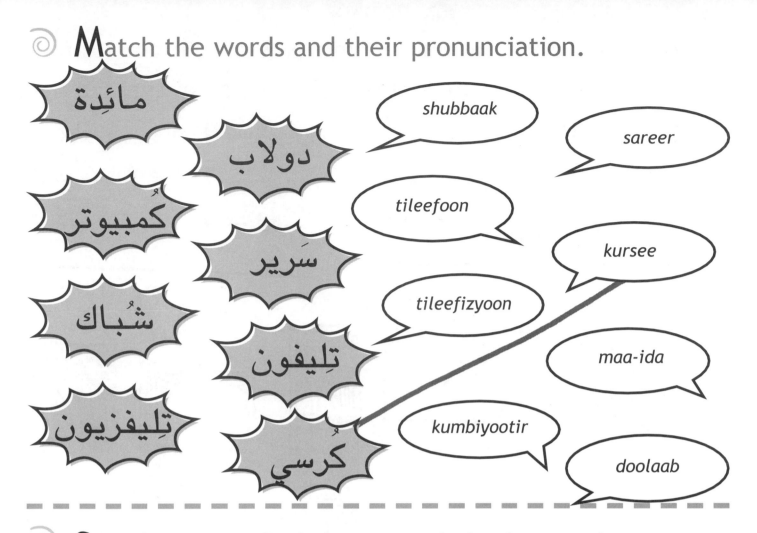

- -

◎ **S**ee if you can find these words in the word square.

The words run *right to left*.

ذ	و	ح	ت ر	ي	ر	س
ط	ة	لا ج	ث	ش	ا	ف
د	ه ت	ز	خ لـ	د	ثـ	
ة	بـ	كنـ	فـ ق	و	ظ	
ك	فـ	سـي	ر ك	ي	مـ	
ن	يـ ا	جـ سـ	نـ	عـ	طـ	
عَ	ن ر فـ	ة	ذ	فـ	و	
ث	فـ	ة غـ	حـ	بـ	ا	بـ

فُرن
سَرير
كُرسي
ثَلاجة
باب
كَنَبة

11

Decide where the household items should go. Then write the correct number in the picture, as in the example.

10 كُمبيوتر	7 دولاب	4 تِليفزيون	1 مائِدة
11 شُباك	8 فُرن	5 تِليفون	2 كُرسي
12 باب	9 ثَلاجة	6 سَرير	3 كَنَبة

Now see if you can fill in the household word at the bottom of the page by choosing the correct Arabic.

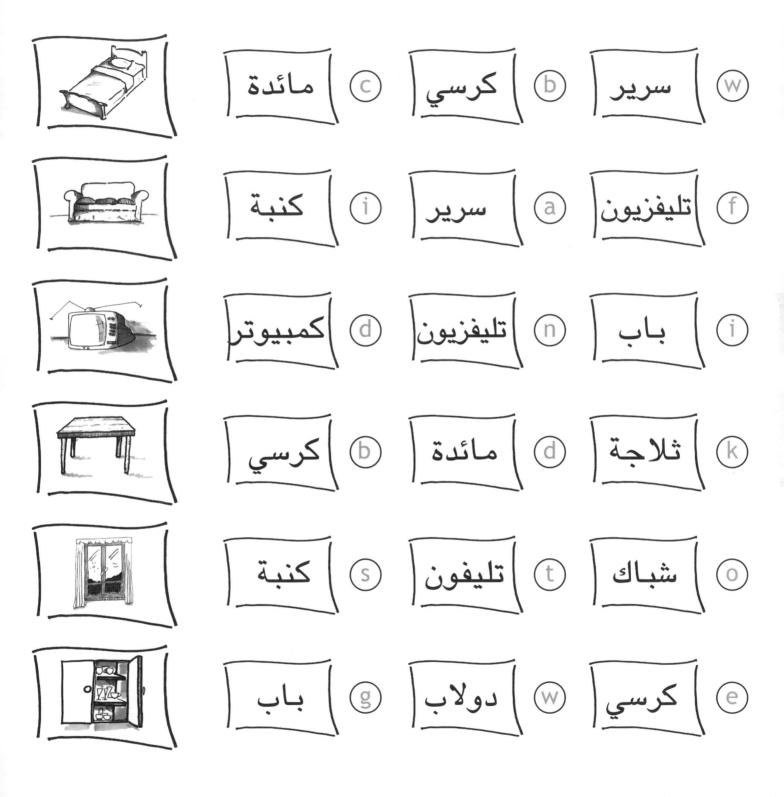

English word: ⓦ ◯ ◯ ◯ ◯ ◯

➋ CLOTHES

Look at the pictures of different clothes.
Tear out the flashcards for this topic.
Follow steps 1 and 2 of the plan in the introduction.

حِزام
Hizaam

بُلوفر
buloofir

شورت
shoort

بَنطلون
banTaloon

جَورَب
jawrab

تي شيرت
tee-sheert

جيبة
jeeba

مِعطَف
mi'Taf

فُستان
fustaan

قُبَّعة
qubba'a

حِذاء *HiTHaa*

قَميص *qamees*

Match the Arabic words and their pronunciation.

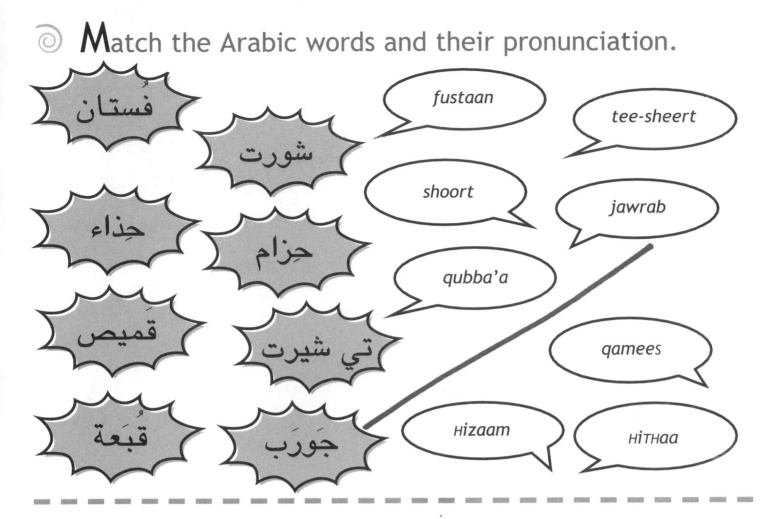

فُستان   شورت

fustaan   *tee-sheert*

shoort   *jawrab*

حِذاء   حِزام

qubba'a

قميص   تي شيرت

qamees

قُبَّعة   جَورَب

ḥizaam   *ḥiṯḥaa*

See if you can find these clothes in the word square.

The words run *right to left*.

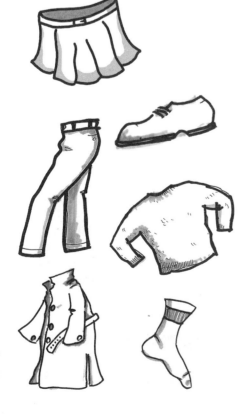

ر	ف	و	ل	ب	ث	ي	ق
ط	ة	لا	ج	ب	ر	و	ج
د	ه	ت	ز	ل	خ	د	ث
ه	ب	ي	ج	ف	ق	و	ظ
ك	ف	ي	س	ر	خ	ي	م
ظ	ي	ن	و	ل	ط	ن	ب
م	ا	ف	ط	ع	م	ف	و
ث	ف	ة	غ	ء	ا	ذ	ح

◎ **N**ow match the Arabic words, their pronunciation, and the English meaning, as in the example.

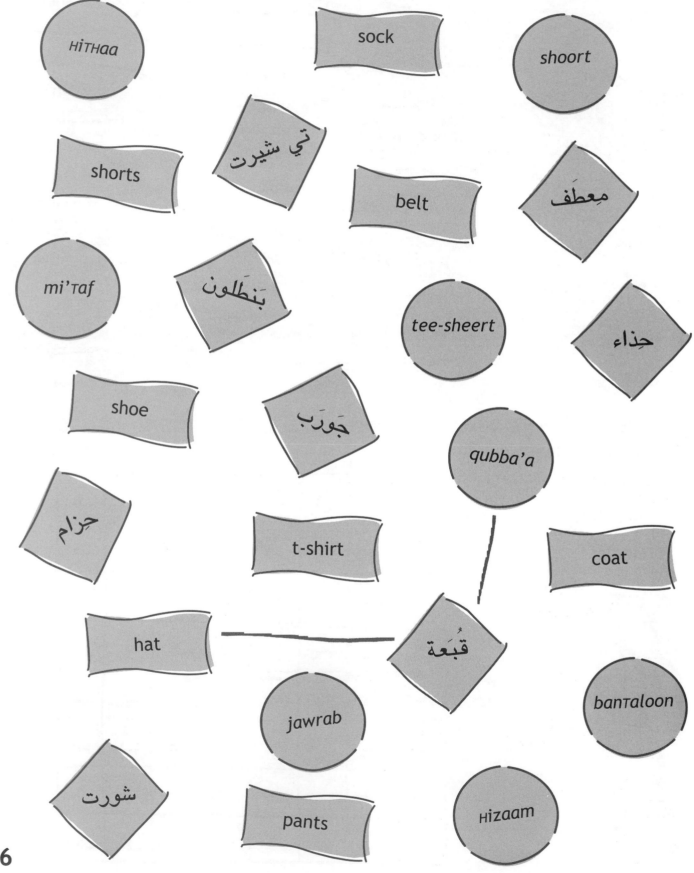

HiTHaa

sock

shoort

shorts

تي شيرت

belt

مِعطَف

mi'Taf

بَنطَلون

tee-sheert

حِذاء

shoe

جَورَب

qubba'a

حِزام

t-shirt

coat

hat

قُبَعة

banTaloon

jawrab

شورت

pants

Hizaam

Candy is going on vacation. Count how many of each type of clothing she is packing in her suitcase.

	قبعة	2		معطف			حزام			حذاء
	بنطلون			شورت			فستان			جورب
	جيبة			تي شيرت			قميص			بلوفر

Someone has ripped up the Arabic words for clothes.
Can you join the two halves of the words, as the example?

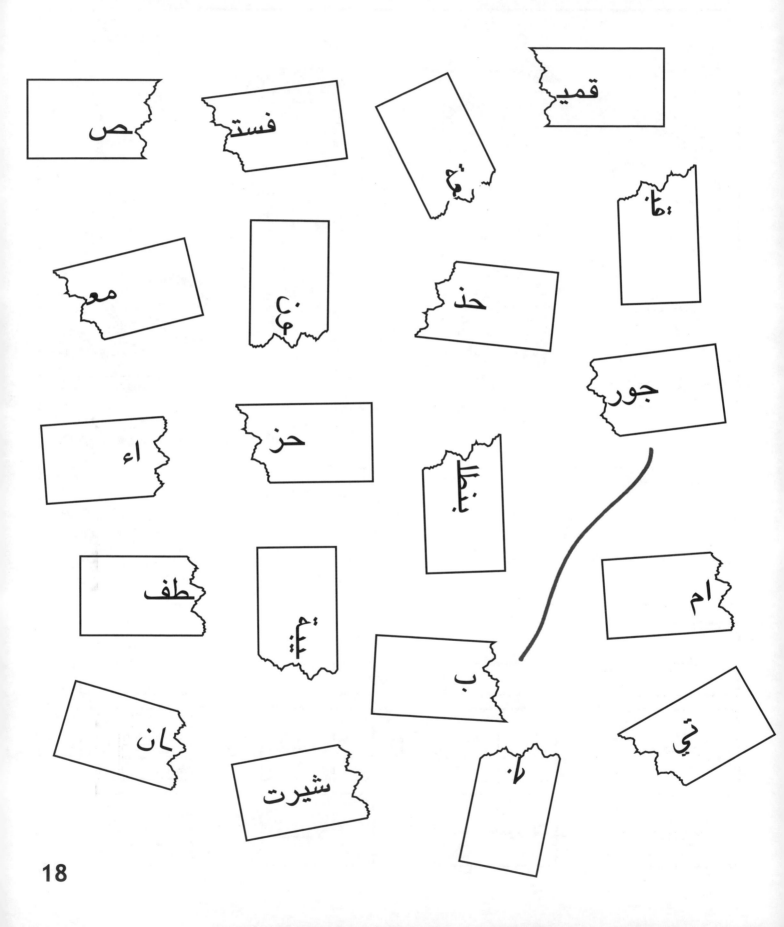

③ AROUND TOWN

Look at the pictures of things you might find around town.
Tear out the flashcards for this topic.
Follow steps 1 and 2 of the plan in the introduction.

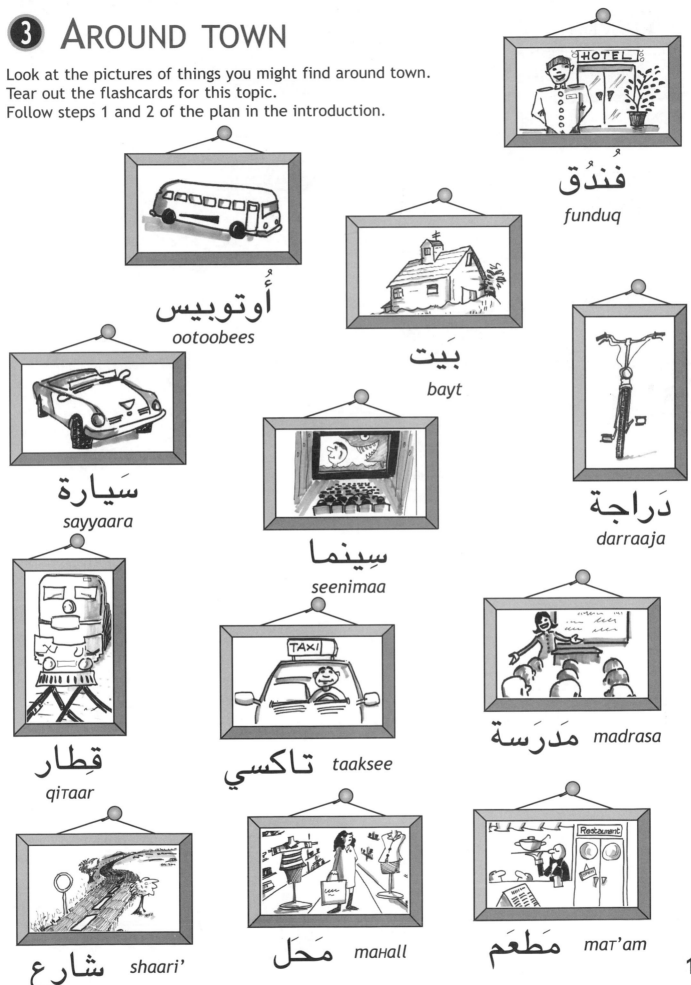

فُنْدُق
funduq

أُوتوبيس
ootoobees

بَيت
bayt

دَراجة
darraaja

سَيارة
sayyaara

سِينما
seenimaa

قِطار
qiṭaar

تاكسي
taaksee

مَدرَسة
madrasa

شارِع
shaari'

مَحَل
maнall

مَطعَم
maт'am

19

◎ **M**atch the Arabic words to their English equivalents.

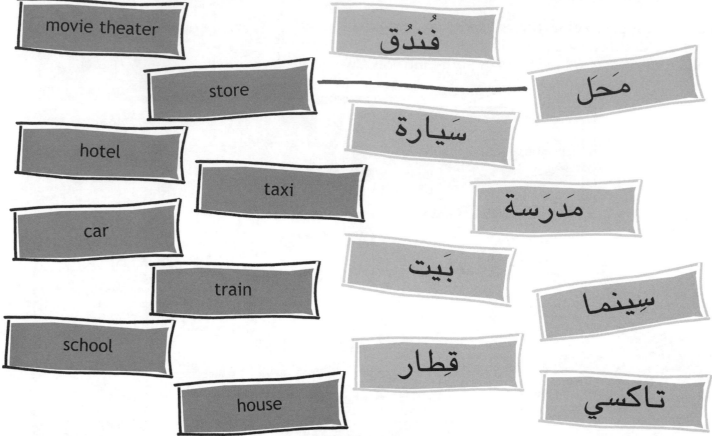

movie theater

store

hotel

taxi

car

train

school

house

فُنْدُق

مَحَل

سَيارة

مَدرَسة

بَيت

سِينما

قِطار

تاكسي

◎ **N**ow list the correct order of the English words to match the Arabic word chain, as in the example.

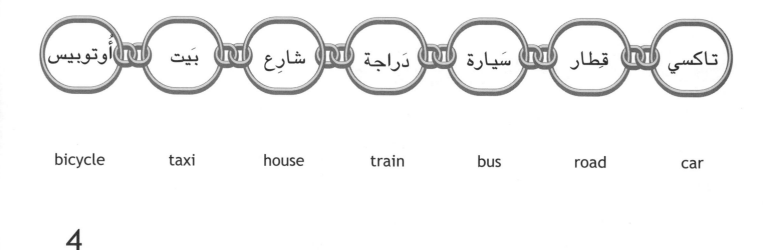

أُوتوبيس بَيت شارِع دَراجة سَيارة قِطار تاكسي

bicycle   taxi   house   train   bus   road   car

4 _____ _____ _____ _____ _____ _____

Match the words to the signs.

مَدرَسة	سَيارة	دَراجة	أُوتوبيس
مَطعَم	قِطار	فُندُق	تاكسي

21

Now choose the Arabic word that matches the picture to fill in the English word at the bottom of the page.

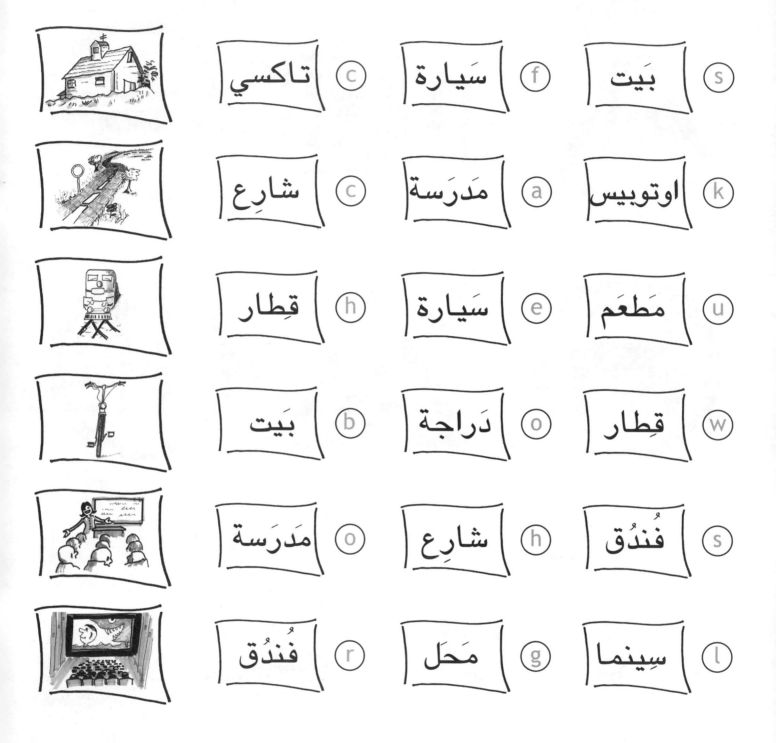

ⓒ تاكْسي	ⓕ سَيَّارة	ⓢ بَيت
ⓒ شارِع	ⓐ مَدرَسة	ⓚ اوتوبيس
ⓗ قِطار	ⓔ سَيَّارة	ⓤ مَطعَم
ⓑ بَيت	ⓞ دَراجة	ⓦ قِطار
ⓞ مَدرَسة	ⓗ شارِع	ⓢ فُندُق
ⓡ فُندُق	ⓖ مَحَل	ⓛ سِينَما

English word: ⓢ ◯ ◯ ◯ ◯ ◯

22

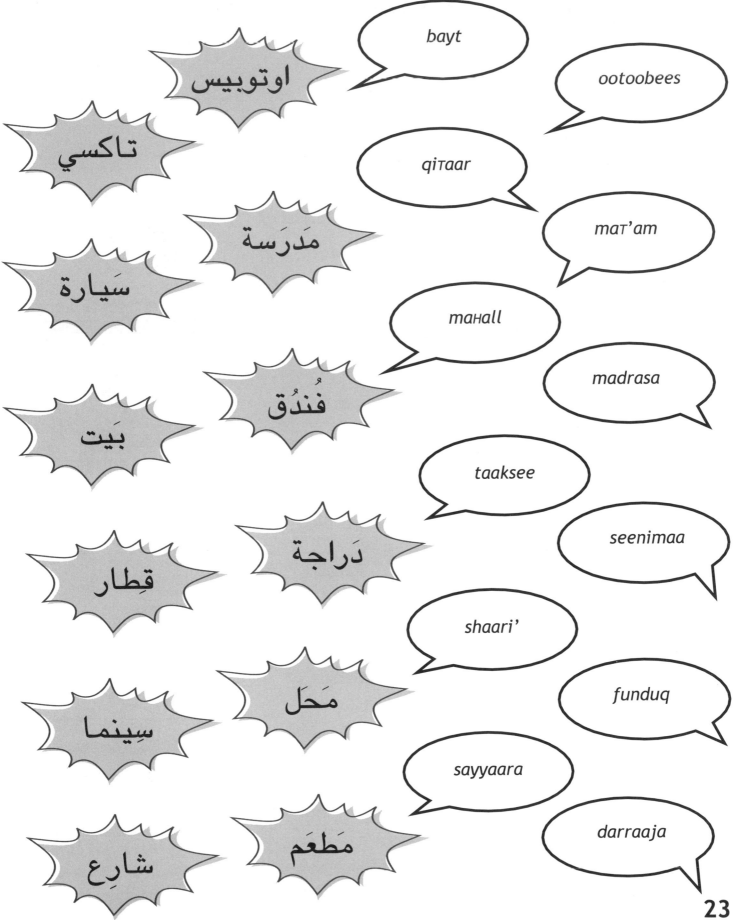

④ COUNTRYSIDE

Look at the pictures of things you might find in the countryside.
Tear out the flashcards for this topic.
Follow steps 1 and 2 of the plan in the introduction.

تل   tal

جِسر
jisr

مَزرَعة
mazra'a

جبَل
jabal

بُحيرة
buhayra

شَجَرة
shajara

وَردة
warda

نَهر   *nahr*

بَحر   *bahr*

حَقل   *haql*

صَحراء   *sahraa*

غابة
ghaaba

Can you match all the countryside words to the pictures?

جَبَل

مَزرَعة

بَحر

غابة

صَحراء

تَل

بُحيرة

جِسر

نَهر

وَردة

شَجَرة

حَقل

Now check (✔) the features you can find in this landscape.

	جِسر ✔		شَجَرة		صَحراء		تَل
	جَبَل		بَحر		حَقل		غابة
	بُحيرة		نَهر		وَردة		مَزرَعة

Match the Arabic words and their pronunciation.

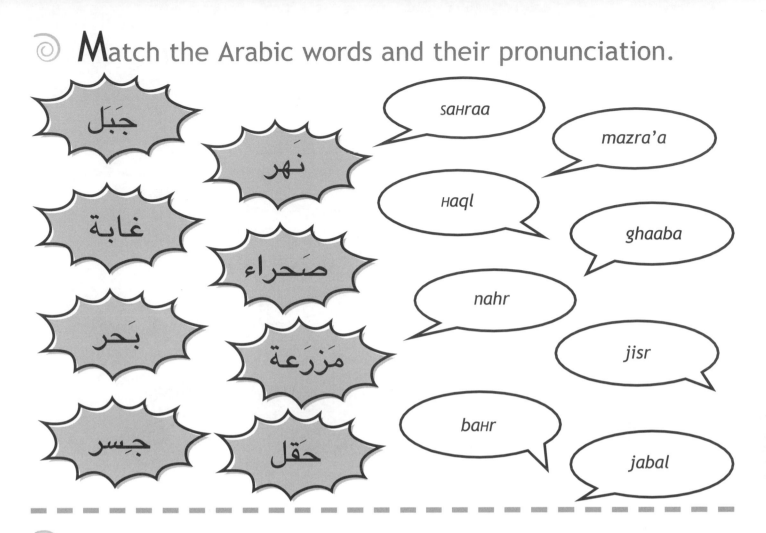

- -

See if you can find these words in the word square.

The words run *right to left*.

ه	فـ	و	سـ	بـ	ثـ	يـ	نـ
ة	ر	جـ	شـ	بـ	خ	و	جـ
د	هـ	تـ	ة	د	ر	و	ثـ
ة	ر	يـ	حـ	بـ	قـ	و	ظ
قـ	يـ	ة	عـ	ر	ز	مـ	ثـ
فـ	يـ	نـ	و	بـ	ظ	ل	تـ
م	ا	غ	طـ	قـ	مـ	فـ	و
ب	مـ	ر	سـ	جـ	ا	ذ	ضـ

شَجَرة
مَزرَعة
تَل
وَردة
جِسر
بُحيرة

27

Finally, test yourself by joining the Arabic words, their pronunciation, and the English meanings, as in the example.

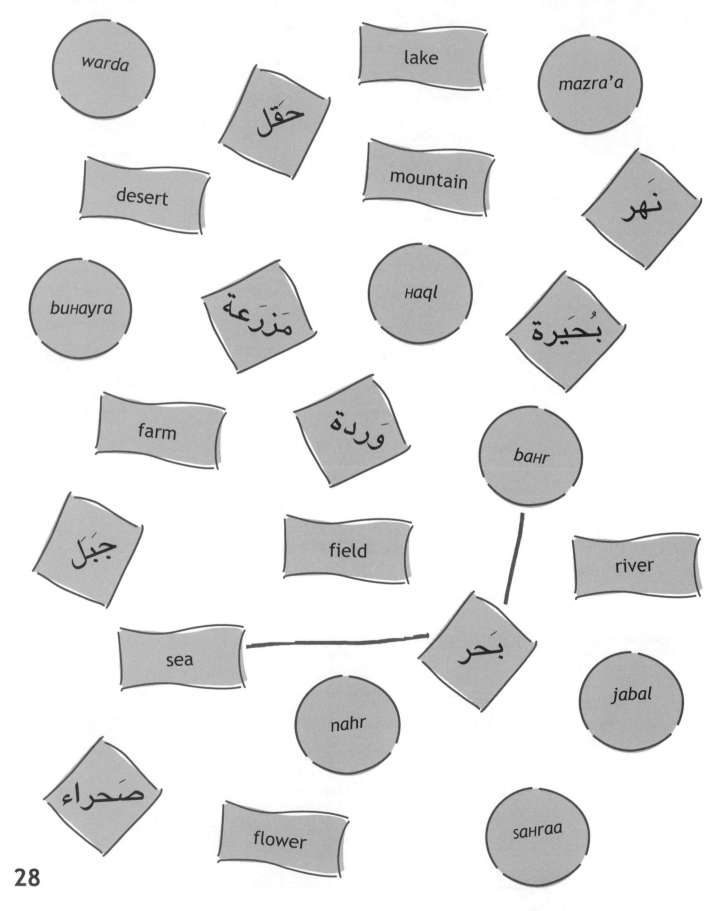

warda

lake

mazra'a

حَقْل

desert

mountain

نَهر

buḥayra

مَزْرَعة

ḥaql

بُحَيرة

farm

وَرْدة

baḥr

جَبَل

field

river

sea

بَحْر

jabal

nahr

صَحْراء

flower

ṣaḥraa

28

⑤ OPPOSITES

Look at the pictures.
Tear out the flashcards for this topic.
Follow steps 1 and 2 of the plan in the introduction.

وَسِخ
wasikh

نَظيف
nazeef

صَغير
sagheer

كَبير
kabeer

رَخيص
rakhees

خَفيف
khafeef

بَطيء
вaтee

غالٍ
ghaalee

ثَقيل
thaqeel

سَريع
saree'

قَديم
qadeem

جَديد
jadeed

29

Join the Arabic words to their English equivalents.

expensive

نَظيف

big

ثَقيل

light

صَغير

slow

قَديم

clean

جَديد

inexpensive ———————— رَخيص

dirty

سَريع

small

بَطيء

heavy

غالٍ

new

وَسِخ

fast

خَفيف

old

كَبير

Now choose the Arabic word that matches the picture to fill in the English word at the bottom of the page.

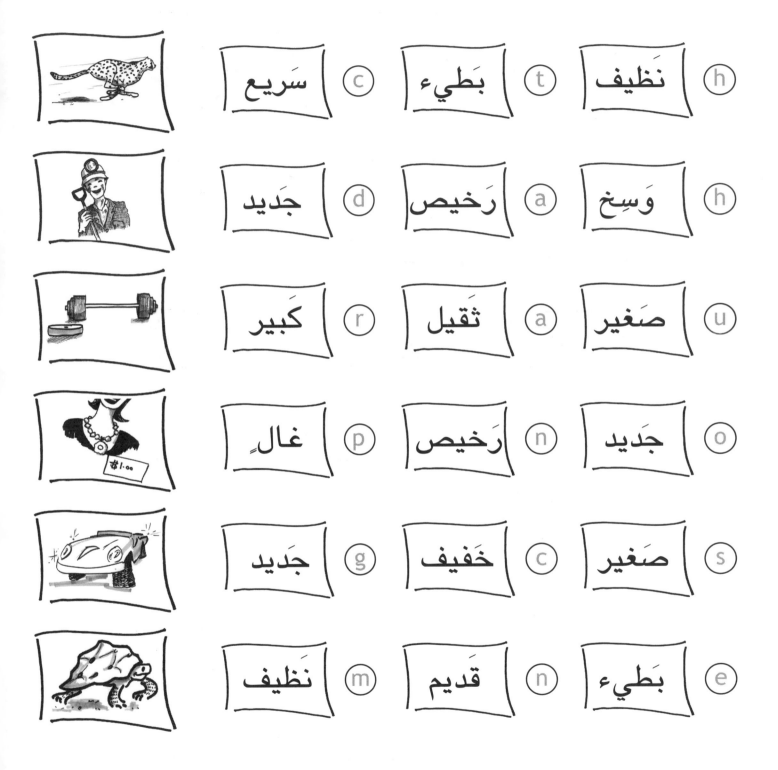

English word: ◯ ◯ ◯ ◯ ◯ ◯

Find the odd one out in these groups of words.

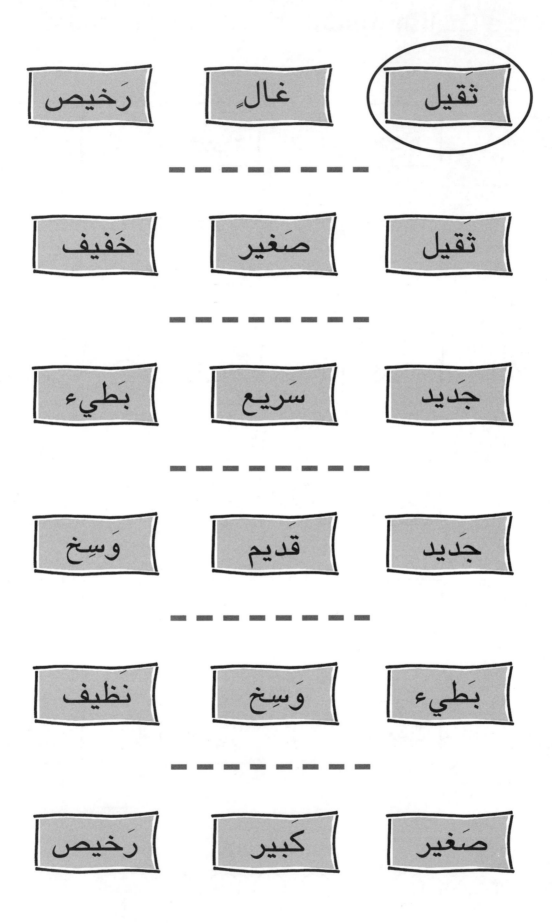

رَخيص	غالِ	ثَقيل

- - - - -

خَفيف	صَغير	ثَقيل

- - - - -

بَطيء	سَريع	جَديد

- - - - -

وَسِخ	قَديم	جَديد

- - - - -

نَظيف	وَسِخ	بطيء

- - - - -

رَخيص	كَبير	صَغير

Finally, join the English words to their Arabic opposites, as in the example.

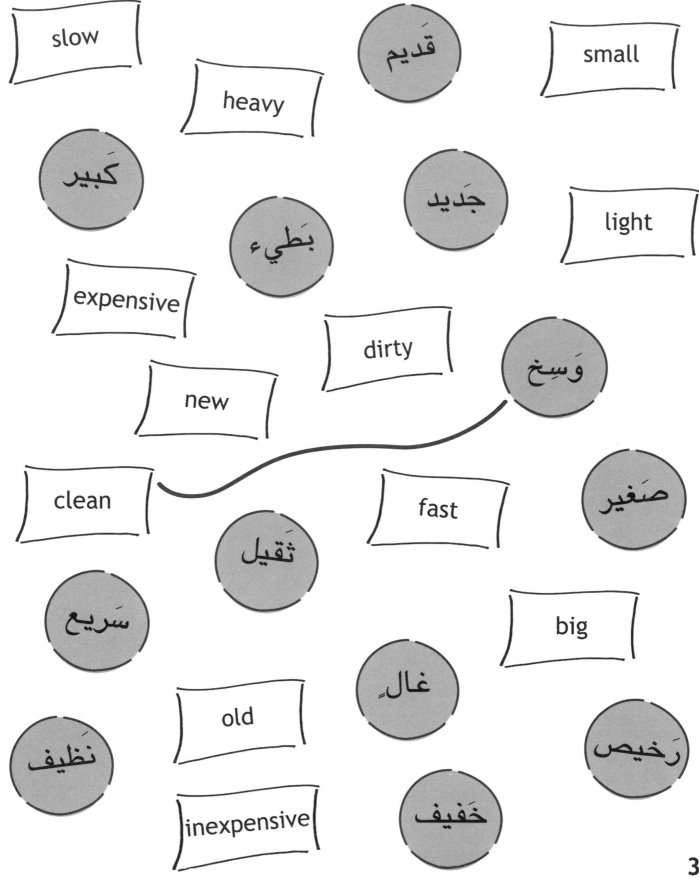

slow

heavy

قَديم

small

كَبير

بَطيء

جَديد

light

expensive

dirty

new

وَسِخ

clean

fast

صَغير

ثَقيل

سَريع

big

نَظيف

old

غالٍ

خَفيف

inexpensive

رَخيص

33

6 ANIMALS

Look at the pictures.
Tear out the flashcards for this topic.
Follow steps 1 and 2 of the plan in the introduction.

بَطة *baтта*

فيل *feel*

قِطة *qiтta*

كَلب *kalb*

أرنَب *arnab*

قِرد *qird*

سَمَكة *samaka*

خَروف *kharoof*

فَأر *faar*

بَقَرة *baqara*

حُصان *Husaan*

أسَد *asad*

34

Match the animals to their associated pictures, as in the example.

أرنَب

حُصان

قِرد

قِطة

خَروف

فأر

كَلب

أسَد

سَمَكة

بقَرة

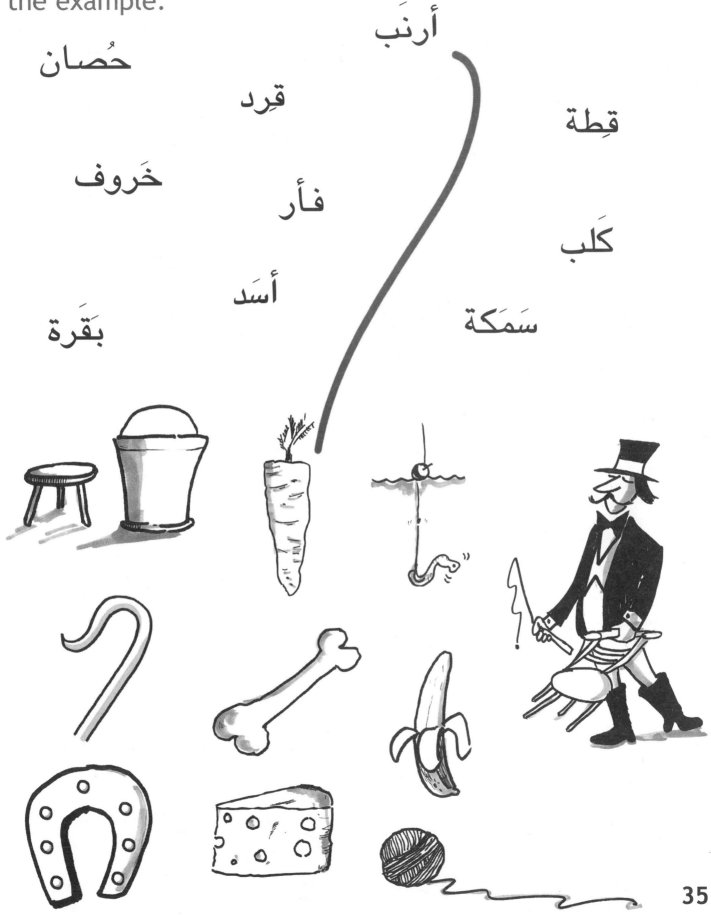

Now match the Arabic to the pronunciation.

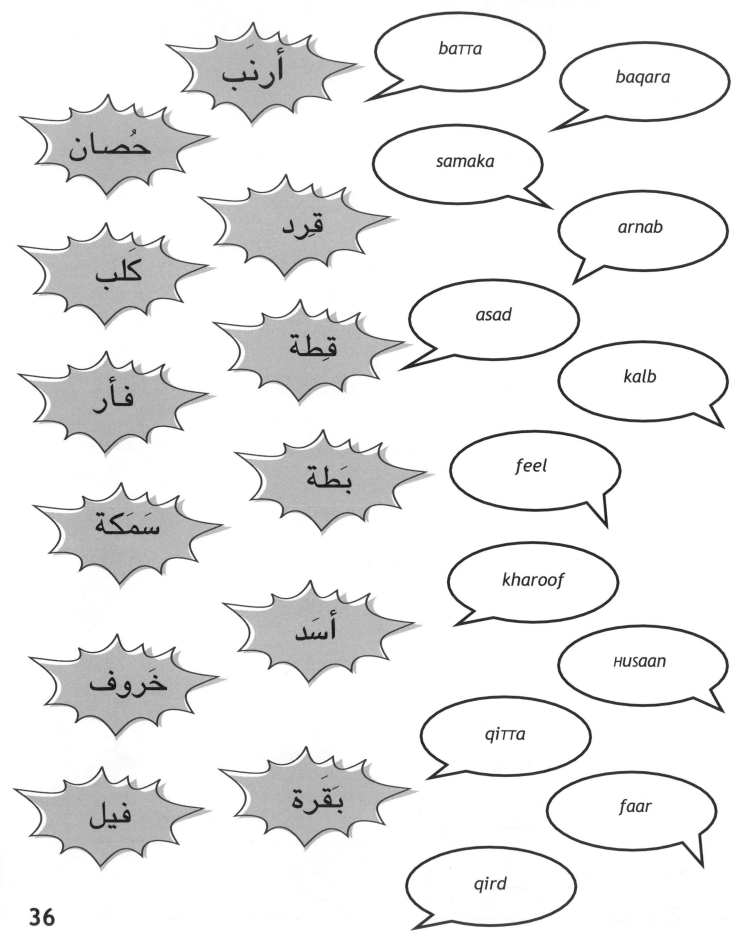

Check (✔) the animal words you can find in the word pile.

بُحَيرة   قِطة   كُرسي   سَيارة

أرنَب   فيل   خَروف   سَرير

ثَقيل   كَنَبة   سينما   حِذاء

تَل   أسَد   بقَرة   سَمَكة

37

Join the Arabic animals to their English equivalents.

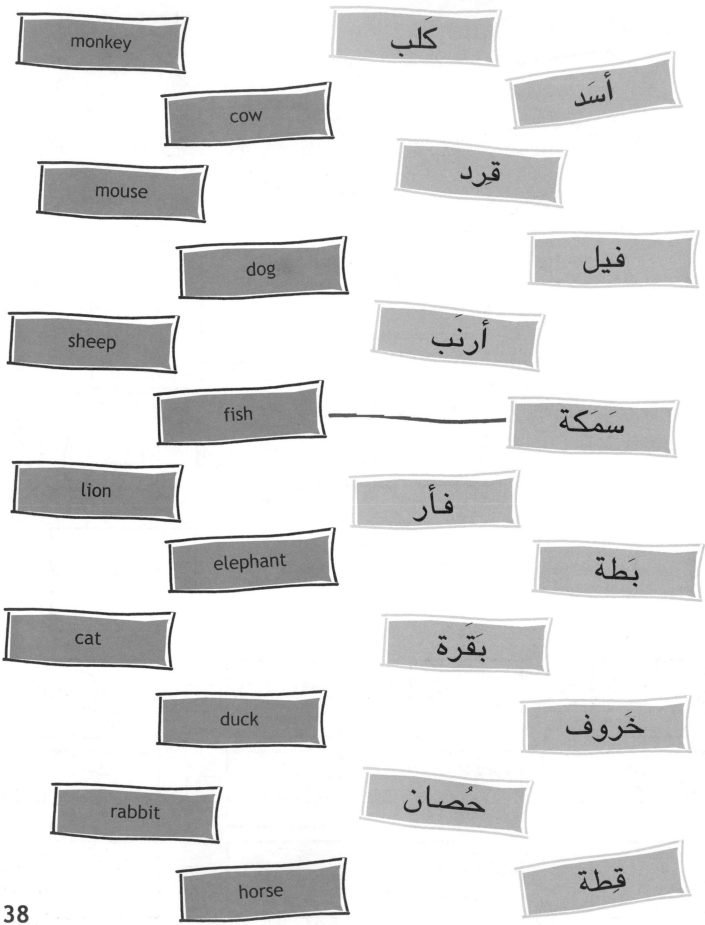

monkey

كَلب

cow

أَسَد

mouse

قِرد

dog

فيل

sheep

أرنَب

fish ————————— سَمَكة

lion

فأر

elephant

بَطة

cat

بقَرة

duck

خَروف

rabbit

حُصان

horse

قِطة

38

⑦ PARTS OF THE BODY

Look at the pictures of parts of the body.
Tear out the flashcards for this topic.
Follow steps 1 and 2 of the plan in the introduction.

إصبَع
isba'

رَأس
ra-as

ذِراع
ᴛʜ*iraa*

عَين
'ayn

ساق
saaq

ظَهر
zahr

يَد
yad

شَعر
sha'r

بَطن
baᴛn

أُذُن
uᴛʜun

أَنف
anf

فَم
fam

Someone has ripped up the Arabic words for parts of the body. Can you join the two halves of the word again?

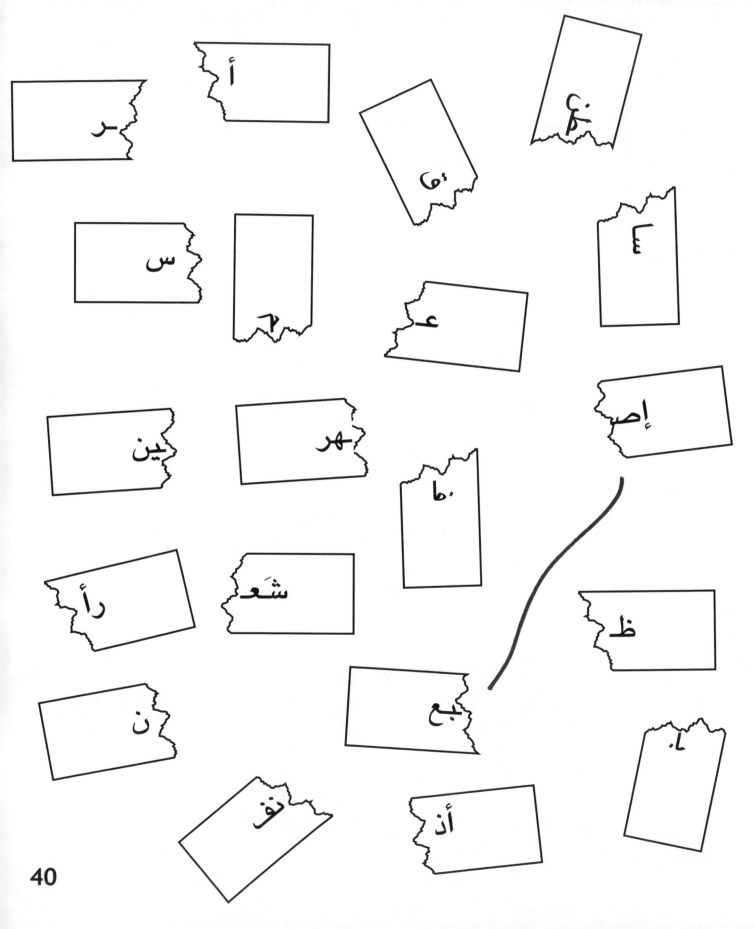

◎ **S**ee if you can find and circle six parts of the body in the word square, then draw them in the boxes below.

The words run *right to left*.

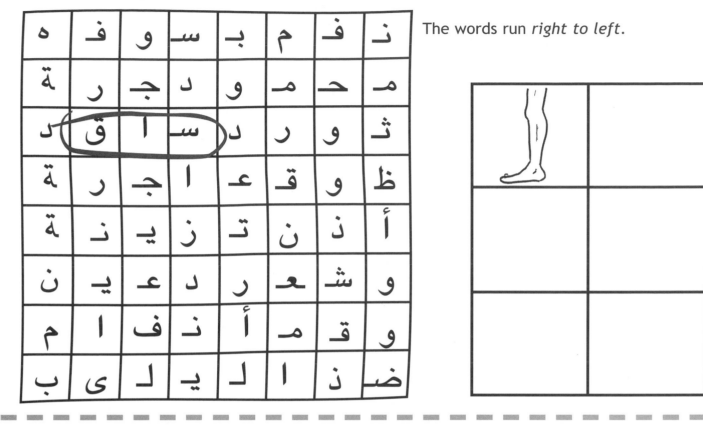

◎ **N**ow match the Arabic to the pronunciation.

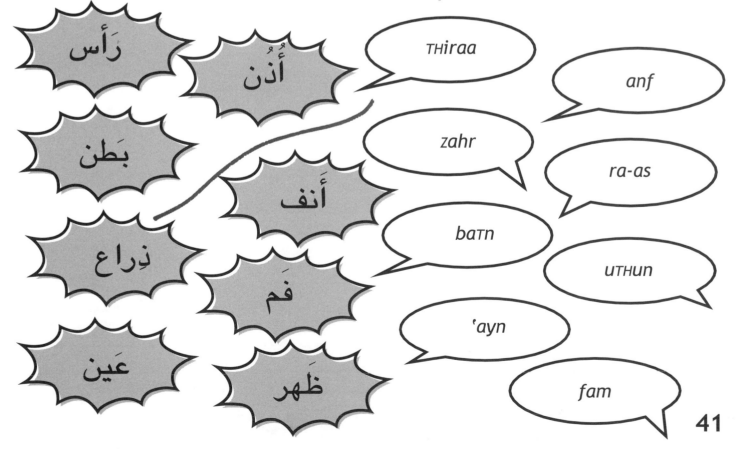

41

Label the body with the correct number, and write the pronunciation next to the words.

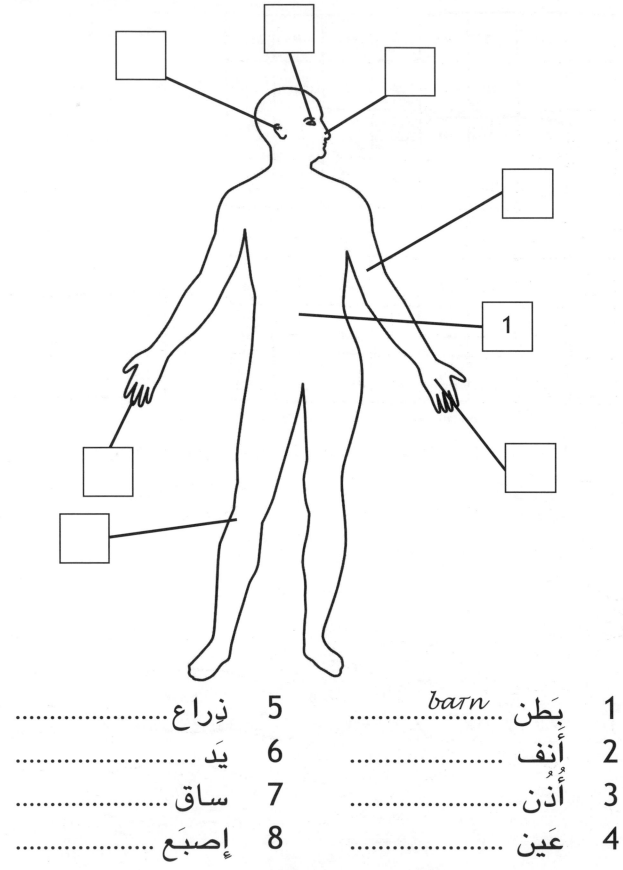

5 ذِراع		1 بَطن .... *baτn*
6 يَد		2 أنف ....
7 ساق		3 أذُن ....
8 إصبَع		4 عَين ....

Finally, match the Arabic words, their pronunciation, and the English meanings, as in the example.

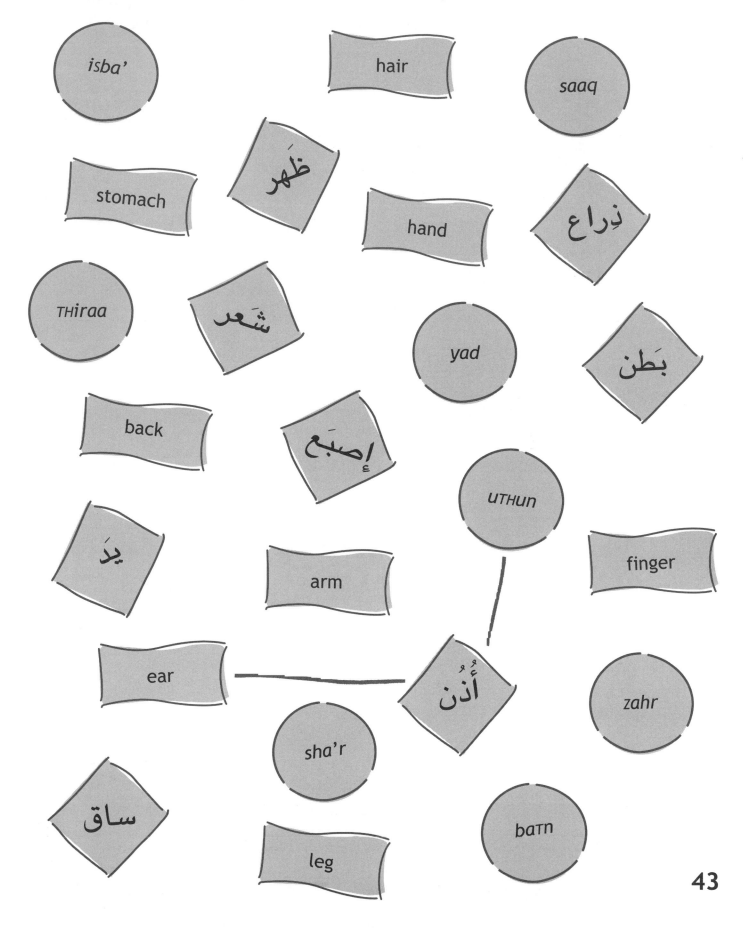

isba'

hair

saaq

stomach

ظَهر

hand

ذِراع

THiraa

شَعر

yad

بَطن

back

إصبَع

uTHun

يَد

arm

finger

ear

أُذُن

zahr

sha'r

ساق

baTn

leg

8 USEFUL EXPRESSIONS

Look at the pictures.
Tear out the flashcards for this topic.
Follow steps 1 and 2 of the plan in the introduction.

لا *laa*

نَعم *na'm*

مَع السَلامة *ma' as-salaama*

أَين؟ *ayn?*

أَهلا *ahlan*

أَمس *ams*

اليَوم *al-yawm*

غَدا *ghadan*

هُنا *huna*

هُناك *hunaak*

الآن *al-aan*

بِكم؟ *bikam?*

آسِف *aasif*

عَظيم *'azeem*

مِن فَضلك *min faɒlak*

شُكرا *shukran*

44

Match the Arabic words to their English equivalents.

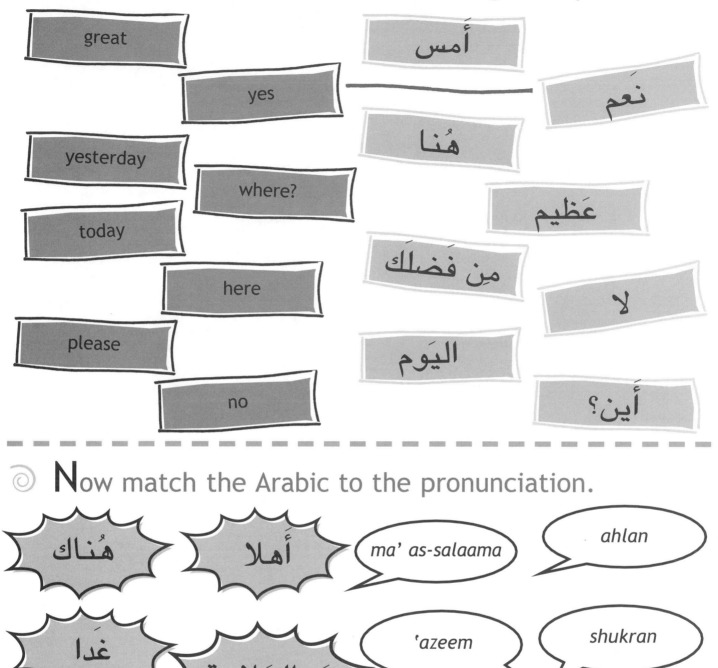

great — عَظيم

yes — نَعَم

yesterday — أمس

where? — أَين؟

today — اليَوم

here — هُنا

please — مِن فَضلَك

no — لا

Now match the Arabic to the pronunciation.

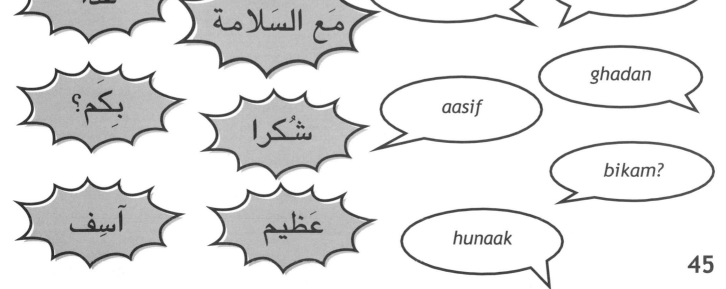

هُناك — أَهلا — ma' as-salaama — ahlan

غَدا — مَع السَلامة — 'azeem — shukran

بِكَم؟ — شُكرا — aasif — ghadan

آسِف — عَظيم — hunaak — bikam?

Choose the Arabic word that matches the picture to
fill in the English word at the bottom of the page.

هُنا ⓟ	لا ⓒ	نَعم ⓣ	
شُكرا ⓙ	آسِف ⓐ	مِن فَضلك ⓛ	
نَعم ⓜ	لا ⓔ	اليَوم ⓘ	
هُناك ⓑ	أَهلا ⓐ	الآن ⓧ	
أَين؟ ⓢ	عَظيم ⓗ	أَمس ⓣ	
أَهلا ⓑ	لا ⓨ	نَعم ⓔ	

English word: ⓟ ◯ ◯ ◯ ◯ ◯

46

What are these people saying? Write the correct number in each speech bubble, as in the example.

7 أَينِ؟	5 هُنا	3 نَعم	1 أَهلا
8 بِكم؟	6 آسِف	4 لا	2 مِن فَضلَك

Finally, match the Arabic words, their pronunciation, and the English meanings, as in the example.

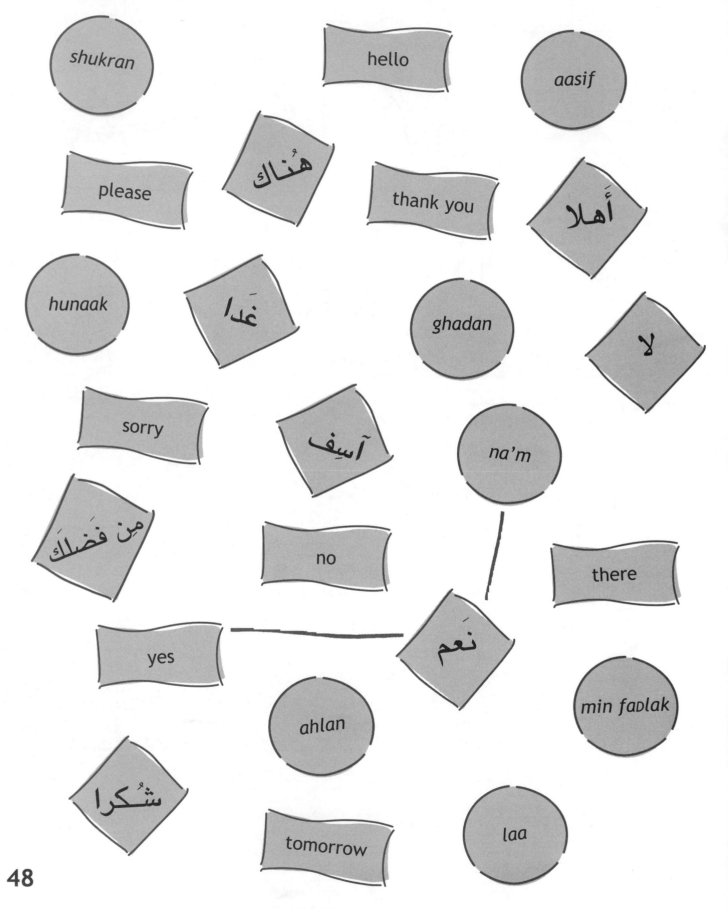

shukran

hello

aasif

هُناك

please

thank you

أَهلا

hunaak

غَدا

ghadan

لا

sorry

آسِف

na'm

مِن فَضلَك

no

there

yes

نَعم

min faɒlak

ahlan

شُكرا

tomorrow

laa

● ROUND-UP

This section is designed to review all the 100 words you have met in the different topics. It is a good idea to test yourself with your flashcards before trying this section.

◎ These ten objects are hidden in the picture. Can you find and circle them?

كرسي	باب	قبعة	دراجة	سمكة
كلب	سرير	جورب	معطف	وردة

See if you can remember all these words.

اليوم

أوتوبيس

سريع

أنف

صحراء

نعم

دولاب

أسد

فستان

رخيص

نهر

ساق

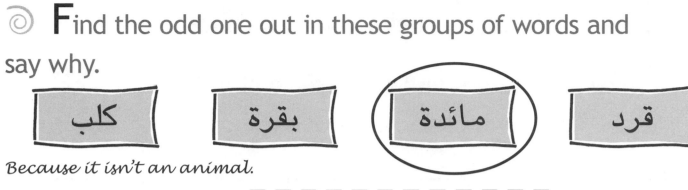

Find the odd one out in these groups of words and say why.

| كلب | بقرة | مائدة | قرد |

Because it isn't an animal.

| سيارة | اوتوبيس | قطار | تليفون |

| مزرعة | معطف | قميص | جيبة |

| بحر | بحيرة | نهر | شجرة |

| غالٍ | وسخ | نظيف | سينما |

| أرنب | قطة | سمكة | أسد |

| ذراع | كنبة | رأس | بطن |

| من فضلك | أمس | اليوم | غدا |

| فرن | سرير | دولاب | ثلاجة |

◎ **L**ook at the objects below for 30 seconds.

◎ **C**over the picture and try to remember all the objects.
Circle the Arabic words for those you remember.

باب   شكرا   حذاء   وردة

قطار   معطف   هنا   لا   سيارة

حصان   كرسي   جبل   حزام

سرير   عين   تي شيرت   جورب

قرد   تليفزيون   تاكسي   شورت

© **N**ow match the Arabic words, their pronunciation, and the English meanings, as in the example.

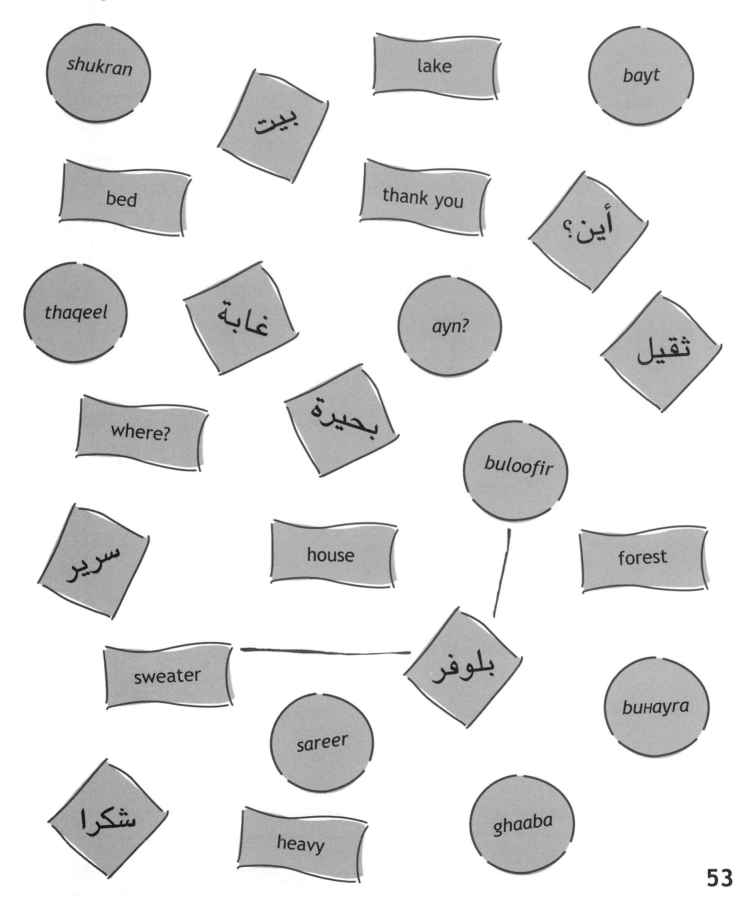

shukran

lake

بيت

bayt

bed

thank you

أين؟

thaqeel

غابة

ayn?

ثقيل

where?

بحيرة

buloofir

سرير

house

forest

sweater

بلوفر

buнayra

sareer

شكرا

ghaaba

heavy

Fill in the English phrase at the bottom of the page.

w) كنبة	g) تاكسي	t) أذن
o) معطف	a) وسخ	e) جسر
m) نعم	l) بكم؟	i) اليوم
b) بقرة	l) شباك	h) مطعم
e) أين؟	a) فم	d) كلب
o) عين	p) مائدة	v) أهلا
n) تل	y) لا	r) اوتوبيس
n) أرنب	e) شارع	s) فرن

54   English phrase: w ◯ ◯ ◯   ◯ ◯ ◯ ◯ !

Look at the two pictures and check (✔) the objects that are different in Picture B.

Picture A

Picture B

 شورت ☐

 تي شيرت ☐

باب ☐

 قطة ☐

 كرسي ☐

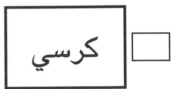 سمكة ☐

 جورب ☐

 كلب ☐

Now join the Arabic words to their English equivalents.

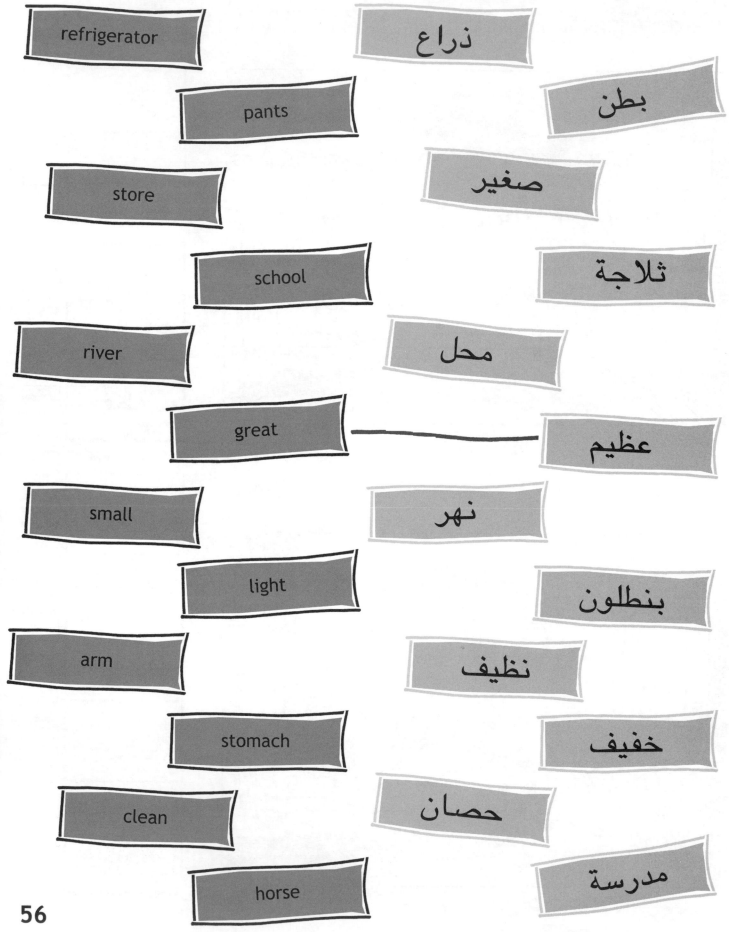

refrigerator

ذراع

pants

بطن

store

صغير

school

ثلاجة

river

محل

great

عظيم

small

نهر

light

بنطلون

arm

نظيف

stomach

خفيف

clean

حصان

horse

مدرسة

Try to match the Arabic to the pronunciation.

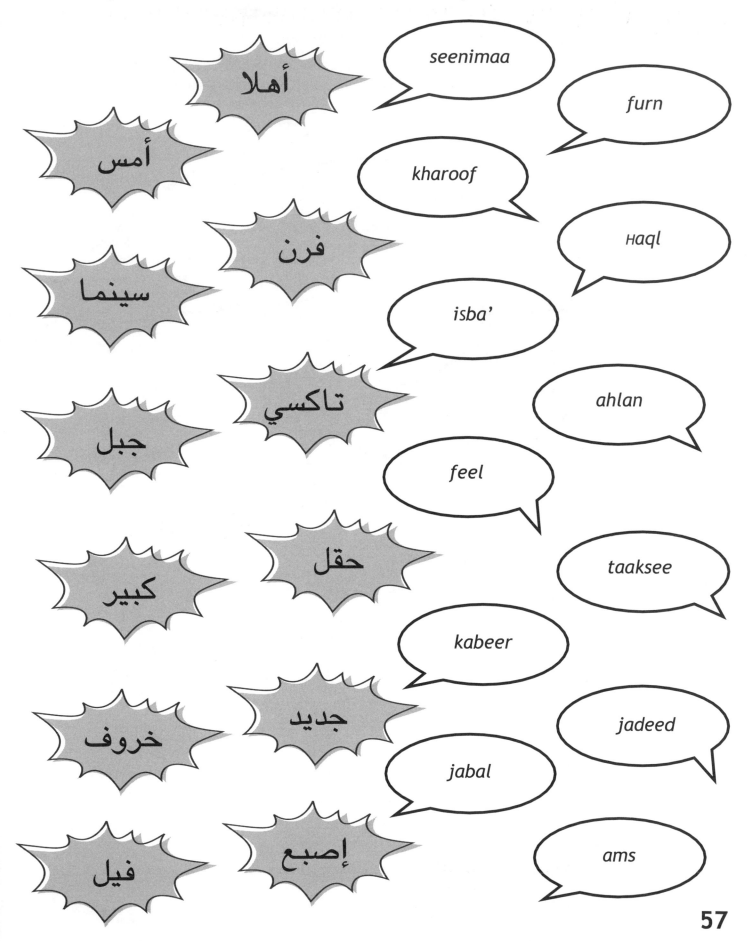

◎ Snake game.

- You will need a die and counter(s). You can challenge yourself to reach the finish or play with someone else. You have to throw the exact number to finish.
- Throw the die and move forward that number of spaces. When you land on a word you must pronounce it and say what it means in English. If you can't, you have to go back to the square you came from.

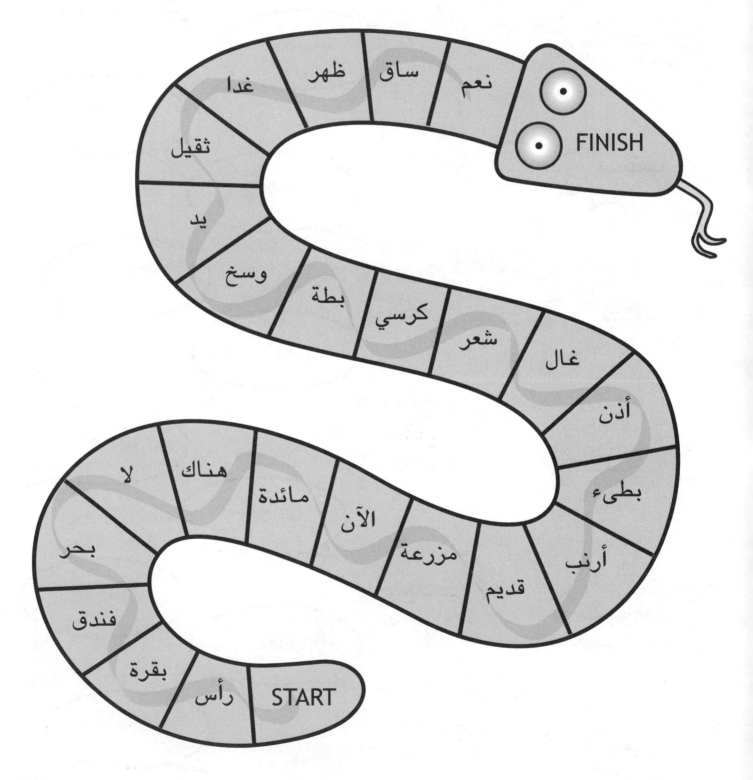

 Answers

❶ AROUND THE HOME

Page 10 (top)
See page 9 for correct picture.

Page 10 (bottom)

door	باب
cupboard	دولاب
stove	فرن
bed	سرير
table	مائدة
chair	كرسي
refrigerator	ثلاجة
computer	كمبيوتر

Page 11 (top)

مائدة	*maa-ida*
دولاب	*doolaab*
كمبيوتر	*kumbiyootir*
سرير	*sareer*
شباك	*shubbaak*
تليفون	*tileefoon*
تليفزيون	*tileefizyoon*
كرسي	*kursee*

Page 11 (bottom)

Page 12

Page 13
English word: window

❷ CLOTHES

Page 15 (top)

فستان	*fustaan*
شورت	*shoort*
حذاء	*ḤITḤaa*
حزام	*ḤIzaam*
قميص	*qamees*
تي شيرت	*tee-sheert*
قبعة	*qubba'a*
جورب	*jawrab*

Page 15 (bottom)

Page 16

hat	قبعة	*qubba'a*
shoe	حذاء	*ḤITḤaa*
sock	جورب	*jawrab*
shorts	شورت	*shoort*
t-shirt	تي شيرت	*tee-sheert*
belt	حزام	*ḤIzaam*
coat	معطف	*mi'Ṭaf*
pants	بنطلون	*banṬaloon*

Page 17

قبعة (hat)	2
معطف (coat)	0
حزام (belt)	2
حذاء (shoe)	2 (1 pair)
بنطلون (pants)	0
شورت (shorts)	2
فستان (dress)	1
جورب (sock)	6 (3 pairs)
جيبة (skirt)	1
تي شيرت (t-shirt)	3
قميص (shirt)	0
بلوفر (sweater)	1

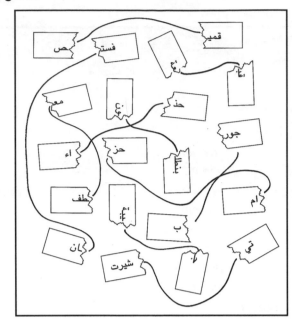

❸ AROUND TOWN

Page 20 (top)

movie theater	سينما
store	محل
hotel	فندق
taxi	تاكسي
car	سيارة
train	قطار
school	مدرسة
house	بيت

Page 20 (bottom)

bicycle	4
taxi	7
house	2
train	6
bus	1
road	3
car	5

Page 21

مدرسة   تاكسي   اوتوبيس

سيارة   قطار   مطعم

فندق   دراجة

Page 22

English word: school

Page 23

اوتوبيس	*ootoobees*
تاكسي	*taaksee*
مدرسة	*madrasa*
سيارة	*sayyaara*
فندق	*funduq*
بيت	*bayt*
دراجة	*darraaja*
قطار	*qiTaar*
محل	*maHall*
سينما	*seenimaa*
مطعم	*maT'am*
شارع	*shaari'*

❹ COUNTRYSIDE

Page 25

See page 24 for correct picture.

Page 26

جسر	✔	حقل	✔
شجرة	✔	غابة	✘
صحراء	✘	بحيرة	✘
تل	✘	نهر	✔
جبل	✔	وردة	✔
بحر	✘	مزرعة	✔

Page 27 (top)

جبل	*jabal*
نهر	*nahr*
غابة	*ghaaba*
صحراء	*saHraa*
بحر	*baHr*
مزرعة	*mazra'a*
جسر	*jisr*
حقل	*Haql*

Page 27 (bottom)

ن	ي	ث	ب	س	و	ف	ه
ة	ر	ج	ش	خ	ب	و	ج
د	ه	ت	د	ر	و	ث	
ر	ي	ح	ب	ق	و	ظ	
ق	ي	ة	ع	ز	م	ث	
ف	ي	د	ن	و	ب	ظ	ل	ت
م	و	غ	ط	ق	ـ	ف	و
ب	م	ر	ج	ا	ذ	ض

Page 28

sea	بحر	*baнr*
lake	بحيرة	*buнayra*
desert	صحراء	*saнraa*
farm	مزرعة	*mazra'a*
flower	وردة	*warda*
mountain	جبل	*jabal*
river	نهر	*nahrr*
field	حقل	*нaql*

⑤ OPPOSITES

Page 30

expensive	غال
big	كبير
light	خفيف
slow	بطىء
clean	نظيف
inexpensive	رخيص
dirty	وسخ
small	صغير
heavy	ثقيل
new	جديد
fast	سريع
old	قديم

Page 31

English word: change

Page 32

Odd one outs are those which are not opposites:

ثقيل

صغير

جديد

وسخ

بطىء

رخيص

Page 33

old	جديد
big	صغير
new	قديم
slow	سريع
dirty	نظيف
small	كبير
heavy	خفيف
clean	وسخ
light	ثقيل
expensive	رخيص
inexpensive	غال

⑥ ANIMALS

Page 35

بقرة	أرنب	سمكة	أسد
خروف	كلب	قرد	
حصان	فأر	قطة	

Page 36

أرنب	*arnab*
حصان	*нusaan*
قرد	*qird*
كلب	*kalb*
قطة	*qiтта*
فأر	*faar*
بطة	*baтта*
سمكة	*samaka*
أسد	*asad*
خروف	*kharoof*
بقرة	*baqara*
فيل	*feel*

Page 37

elephant	✔	mouse	✗
monkey	✗	cat	✔
sheep	✔	dog	✗
lion	✔	cow	✔
fish	✔	horse	✗
duck	✗	rabbit	✔

Page 38

monkey	قرد
cow	بقرة
mouse	فأر
dog	كلب
sheep	خروف
fish	سمكة
lion	أسد
elephant	فيل
cat	قطة
duck	بطة
rabbit	أرنب
horse	حصان

❼ PARTS OF THE BODY

Page 40

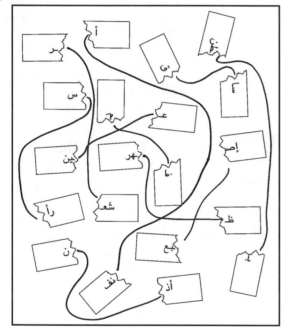

Page 41 (top)

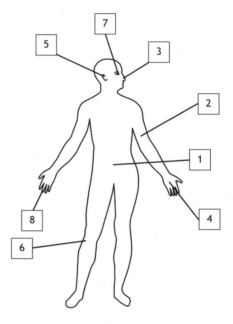

You should have also drawn pictures of:

leg; mouth; ear; nose; eye; hair

Page 41 (bottom)

رأس		ra-as
أذن		UTHUN
بطن		baTn
أنف		anf
ذراع		THiraa
فم		fam
عين		'ayn
ظهر		zahr

Page 42

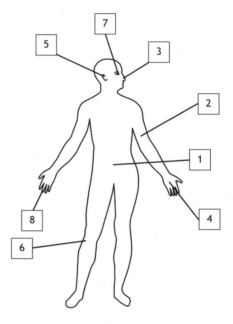

1.	بطن	baTn
2.	ذراع	THiraa
3.	أنف	anf
4.	يد	yad
5.	أذن	UTHUN
6.	ساق	saaq
7.	عين	'ayn
8.	أصبع	isba'

Page 43

ear	أذن	UTHUN
hair	شعر	sha'r
hand	يد	yad
stomach	بطن	baTn
arm	ذراع	THiraa
back	ظهر	zahr
finger	أصبع	isba'
leg	ساق	saaq

❽ USEFUL EXPRESSIONS

Page 45 (top)

great	عظيم
yes	نعم
yesterday	أمس
where?	أين؟
today	اليوم
here	هنا
please	من فضلك
no	لا

Page 45 (bottom)

هناك	*hunaak*
أهلا	*ahlan*
غدا	*ghadan*
مع السلامة	*ma' as-salaama*
بكم؟	*bikam?*
شكرا	*shukran*
آسف	*aasif*
عظيم	*'azeem*

Page 46

English word: please

Page 47

Page 48

yes	نعم	*na'm*
hello	أهلا	*ahlan*
no	لا	*laa*
sorry	آسف	*aasif*
please	من فضلك	*min faᴅlak*
there	هناك	*hunaak*
thank you	شكرا	*shukran*
tomorrow	غدا	*ghadan*

⬤ ROUND-UP

Page 49

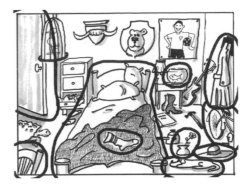

Page 50

صحراء =   أسد =

نعم =   دولاب =   رخيص =

اليوم =   نهر =

أنف =   فستان =   ساق =

سريع =   أتوبيس =

Page 51

مائدة (Because it isn't an animal.)

تليفون (Because it isn't a means of transportation.)

مزرعة (Because it isn't an item of clothing.)

شجرة (Because it isn't connected with water.)

سينما (Because it isn't a descriptive word.)

سمكة (Because it lives in water/doesn't have legs.)

كنبة (Because it isn't a part of the body.)

من فضلك (Because it isn't an expression of time.)

سرير (Because you wouldn't find it in the kitchen.)

Page 52

Words that appear in the picture:

تي شيرت

سيارة

وردة

حذاء

قطار

قرد

تليفزيون

كرسي

حزام

شورت

Page 53

sweater	بلوفر	*buloofir*
lake	بحيرة	*buнayra*
thank you	شكرا	*shukran*
bed	سرير	*sareer*
house	بيت	*bayt*
forest	غابة	*ghaaba*
where?	أين؟	*ayn*
heavy	ثقيل	*thaqeel*

Page 54

English phrase: well done!

Page 55

شورت	✔ (shade)
تي شيرت	✘
باب	✔ (handle)
قطة	✘
كرسي	✔ (back)
سمكة	✔ (direction)
جورب	✔ (pattern)
كلب	✘

Page 56

refrigerator	ثلاجة
pants	بنطلون
store	محل
school	مدرسة
river	نهر
great	عظيم
small	صغير
light	خفيف
arm	ذراع
stomach	بطن
clean	نظيف
horse	حصان

Page 57

أهلا	*ahlan*
أمس	*ams*
فرن	*furn*
سينما	*seenimaa*
تاكسي	*taaksee*
جبل	*jabal*
حقل	*наql*
كبير	*kabeer*
جديد	*jadeed*
خروف	*kharoof*
إصبع	*isba'*
فيل	*feel*

Page 58

Here are the English equivalents and pronunciation of the words, in order from START to FINISH:

head *ra-as*	farm *mazra'a*	duck *baтта*
cow *baqara*	old *qadeem*	dirty *wasikh*
hotel *funduq*	rabbit *arnab*	hand *yad*
sea *baнr*	slow *baтee*	heavy *thaqeel*
no *laa*	ear *uтнun*	tomorrow *ghadan*
there *hunaak*	expensive *ghalee*	back *zahr*
table *maa-ida*	hair *sha'r*	leg *saaq*
now *al-aan*	chair *kursee*	yes *na'm*

كمبيوتر

kumbiyootir

شبـاك

shubbaak

مائدة

maa-ida

دولاب

doolaab

ثلاجة

thallaaja

كرسي

kursee

كنبة

kanaba

فرن

furn

باب

baab

سرير

sareer

تليفون

tileefoon

تليفزيون

tileefizyoon

window	computer
cupboard	table
chair	refrigerator
stove	sofa
bed	door
television	telephone

حزام

ḥizaam

معطف

mi'Taf

جيبة

jeeba

قبعة

qubba'a

تي شيرت

tee-sheert

حذاء

ḥiTHaa

بلوفر

buloofir

قميص

qamees

شورت

shoorт

جورب

jawrab

بنطلون

banтaloon

فستان

fustaan

coat	belt
hat	skirt
shoe	t-shirt
shirt	sweater
sock	shorts
dress	pants

مدرسة

madrasa

سيارة

sayyaara

شارع

shaari'

سينما

seenimaa

فندق

funduq

محل

maHall

تاكسي

taaksee

دراجة

darraaja

مطعم

maт'am

أوتوبيس

ootoobees

قطار

qiтaar

بيت

bayt

car	school
movie theater	road
store	hotel
bicycle	taxi
bus	restaurant
house	train

بحيرة

buhayra

غابة

ghaaba

تل

tal

بحر

bahr

جبل

jabal

شجرة

shajara

صحراء

sahraa

وردة

warda

جسر

jisr

نهر

nahr

مزرعة

mazra'a

حقل

haql

forest	lake
sea	hill
tree	mountain
flower	desert
river	bridge
field	farm

خفيف

khafeef

ثقيل

thaqeel

صغير

sagheer

كبير

kabeer

جديد

jadeed

قديم

qadeem

بطيء

baтee

سريع

saree'

وسخ

wasikh

نظيف

nazeef

غالٍ

ghaalee

رخيص

rakhees

light	heavy
small	big
new	old
slow	fast
dirty	clean
expensive	cheap

بطة

baтта

قطة

qiтта

فأر

faar

بقرة

baqara

أرنب

arnab

كلب

kalb

حصان

Husaan

قرد

qird

أسد

asad

سمكة

samaka

فيل

feel

خروف

kharoof

cat	duck
cow	mouse
dog	rabbit
monkey	horse
fish	lion
sheep	elephant

ذراع *THiraa'*	إصبع *isba'*
رأس *ra-as*	فم *fam*
أذن *uTHun*	ساق *saaq*
يد *yad*	بطن *baTn*
عين *'ayn*	شعر *sha'r*
أنف *anf*	ظهر *zahr*

finger

arm

mouth

head

leg

ear

stomach

hand

hair

eye

back

nose

من فضلك	شكرا
min faɒlak	*shukran*

نعم	لا
na'm	*laa*

أهلا	مع السلامة
ahlan	*ma' as-salaama*

أمس	اليوم
ams	*al-yaum*

غداً	أين؟
ghadan	*ayn*

هنا	هناك
huna	*hunaak*

آسف	بكم؟
aasif	*bikam*

عظيم!	الآن
'azeem	*al-aan*

thank you	please
no	yes
goodbye	hello
today	yesterday
where?	tomorrow
there	here
how much?	sorry!
now	great!